W9-BCU-568

JUST **10** MINUTES

JUST **10** MINUTES

Love Food™ is an imprint of
Parragon Books Ltd

Parragon
Queen Street House
4 Queen Street
Bath BA1 1HE, UK

Copyright © Parragon Books Ltd 2007

Love Food™ and the accompanying heart
device is a trademark of Parragon Books Ltd

Design: Terry Jeavons & Company
Photographer: Mike Cooper
Home economist: Lincoln Jefferson

ISBN 978-1-4054-8778-8

All rights reserved. No part of this
publication may be reproduced, stored in
a retrieval system or transmitted, in any form
or by any means, electronic, mechanical,
photocopying, recording, or otherwise, without
the prior permission of the copyright holder.

Printed in China

This book uses imperial, metric, or US cup
measurements. Follow the same units of
measurement throughout; do not mix imperial
and metric. All spoon measurements are level,
unless otherwise stated: teaspoons
are assumed to be 5ml, and tablespoons
are assumed to be 15ml. Unless otherwise
stated, milk is assumed to be whole, eggs
and individual fruits such as bananas are
medium, and pepper is freshly ground
black pepper.

Recipes using raw or very lightly cooked eggs
should be avoided by children, the elderly,
pregnant women, convalescents, and anyone
suffering from an illness. Pregnant and
breast-feeding women are advised to avoid
eating peanuts and peanut products.

Contents

Introduction

If you don't have the time or the inclination to spend a lot of time in the kitchen, but enjoy fresh, tasty wholesome food and creative cooking, then these recipes are for you. All the recipes take just ten minutes (or less) to make. They are full of flavor and goodness, but take little time and effort, as the food is prepared and cooked very quickly.

Convenience foods and ready meals are expensive, often boring, and usually have a bland or "artificial" flavor designed to appeal to a mass market. More importantly they are frequently loaded with preservatives. But "fast" food doesn't have to mean a cocktail of nasty chemicals. You can cook fresh meals quickly with minimum fuss but maximum flavor and, of course, you'll know exactly what has gone into them.

The keys to success are using top quality foods; always choose the freshest and best quality produce for optimum flavor, such as free-range eggs, vibrant fruit and vegetables free from blemishes and bruises, fresh herbs, extra virgin olive oil, and so on. A well-stocked pantry and good utensils make cooking much easier, and basic staples should include rice and pasta. Dried pasta will keep longer than fresh; it comes in a variety of shapes and sizes, and cooks in minutes. Good seasoning is particularly important when food is cooked for a short time, so a stock of good wine vinegar, honey, spices, herbs, and sauces, such as Tabasco and Worcestershire are invaluable to use in recipes to add interest and variety. Canned fish (sardines, anchovies, tuna), tomatoes, corn, and beans are also excellent to keep in the cupboard and you can use these old favorites to add a new imaginative twist to recipes. Cream and yogurt are wonderfully versatile ingredients, perfect for pouring, whisking, and spooning, and will add a richness to sweet and savory dishes. In the freezer, ready-rolled pie dough and good quality ice cream are ideal standbys.

The right tools for the job will make all the difference and will also speed up preparation. Nonstick pans, sharp knives, a couple of whisks, a colander, zester, strainer, wooden spoons and spatulas will all reduce time spent in the kitchen. A food processor or blender is also essential.

There's no fiddly preparation in any of these recipes—no elaborate trimmings, fancy decorations or garnishes—just simple food that looks and tastes fabulous. There is nothing better or more delicious than making your own meals, so try these trouble-free, straightforward recipes and taste the difference.

1 Meat

Prime cuts of meat are best suited to fast cooking. A shortcut that will save you time is to freeze the meat, if possible, so that it will easily cut into wafer-thin slices, if wanted. When broiling, turn the meat only once during cooking for a juicier result.

Orange & Lemon-Coated Crispy Lamb Chops

INGREDIENTS

1 garlic clove, crushed

1 tbsp olive oil

2 tbsp finely grated orange zest

2 tbsp finely grated lemon zest

6 lamb chops

salt and pepper

orange wedges, to garnish

serves ❷

1 Preheat the broiler. Mix the garlic, oil, grated orange and lemon zest, and seasoning together in a bowl.

2 Brush the mixture over the lamb chops and cook under the broiler for 4 to 5 minutes on each side. Serve, garnished with the orange wedges.

Herbed Lamb Burgers

INGREDIENTS

1 lb/450 g fresh lean ground lamb

1½ cups fresh breadcrumbs

1 onion, finely chopped

3 tbsp chopped fresh herbs, such as mint, rosemary, or thyme

1 egg

½ tbsp apple juice

salt and pepper

1 tbsp sunflower or olive oil

4 soft white rolls

lettuce and sliced tomato, to garnish

serves ❹

1 Preheat the broiler or light the barbecue if using. Mix the ground lamb, breadcrumbs, onion, chopped herbs, egg, apple juice, and salt and pepper together in a large bowl.

2 Divide the mixture into 4 burgers and lightly brush with the oil.

3 Broil or barbecue the burgers for 3 to 4 minutes on each side.

4 Serve the herbed lamb burgers inside soft white rolls and garnish with lettuce and sliced tomato.

Teriyaki Steak

INGREDIENTS

four 5½ oz/150 g beef steaks

salt and pepper

2 tbsp vegetable oil

heaping 1¼ cups bean sprouts, trimmed

4 scallions, trimmed and finely sliced

FOR THE TERIYAKI SAUCE

2 tbsp mirin (Japanese rice wine)

2 tbsp sake or pale dry sherry

4 tbsp dark soy sauce

1 tsp granulated or superfine sugar

serves ❹

1 Season the steaks with salt and pepper and set aside.

2 To make the sauce, combine the mirin, sake, soy sauce, and sugar in a bowl, stirring well.

3 Heat 1 tablespoon of oil in a skillet over high heat. Add the bean sprouts and sauté quickly, tossing them in the hot oil for 30 seconds. Remove from the skillet and drain on paper towels.

4 Add the remaining oil to the skillet and when hot add the steaks. Cook for 1 to 3 minutes on each side, according to how rare you like your meat. Remove from the skillet and keep warm.

5 Remove the skillet from the heat and add the sauce and scallions. Return to the heat and simmer for 2 minutes, stirring until the sauce thickens slightly and is glossy.

6 Slice each steak and arrange on a bed of bean sprouts. Spoon over the sauce and serve immediately.

Vietnamese Beef Soup

INGREDIENTS

5 cups good quality beef stock

1 small fresh chile, chopped

1 cinnamon stick

2 star anise

2 cloves

8 oz/225 g porterhouse or tenderloin steak, cut into thin strips

10½ oz/300 g rice noodles

4 tbsp chopped fresh cilantro

lime wedges, to garnish

serves ❷

1 Heat the stock, chile, and spices in a pan until boiling, then reduce the heat and simmer for about 5 minutes.

2 Add the beef strips and simmer for an additional 2 to 3 minutes until cooked to your liking.

3 Cook the noodles according to the package directions, then drain and place in 2 individual serving bowls.

4 Pour over the broth and sprinkle with chopped cilantro. Garnish with lime wedges and serve.

Stir-Fried Beef with Cashew Nuts

INGREDIENTS

2 tbsp sunflower or olive oil

1 lb/450 g top round steak, cut into thin strips

1 tbsp black peppercorns, crushed

2 fresh chiles, seeded and finely chopped

bunch of scallions, trimmed and thinly sliced or chopped

¾ cups cashew nuts

FOR THE SAUCE

3 tbsp soy sauce

2 tbsp rice wine or dry sherry

1 tbsp dark brown sugar

1 tsp five spice powder

serves ❷

1 Heat the oil in a preheated wok until smoking. Add the steak strips, crushed peppercorns, chiles, and scallions and cook for 3 to 4 minutes, tossing the wok to cook evenly.

2 Mix all the ingredients for the sauce together in a bowl and pour into the wok. Cook for 3 minutes, tossing the ingredients until everything is heated through.

3 Add the cashew nuts and toss to combine. Serve immediately.

Peppered Steaks in Whisky Cream Sauce

INGREDIENTS

3 tbsp black peppercorns, crushed

four 6 oz/175 g minute steaks

2 tbsp sunflower or olive oil

8 baby carrots, freshly cooked

fresh flat-leaf parsley sprigs, to garnish

FOR THE WHISKY CREAM SAUCE

2/3 cup heavy cream

2 tbsp beef stock

2–3 tbsp malt whisky

serves 4

1 Press the crushed peppercorns firmly into the steaks to coat.

2 Heat the oil in a skillet and when hot, place the steaks in the skillet and cook for 1 minute on each side.

3 Remove the steaks and keep warm. Pour off the oil from the skillet.

4 Mix the cream, stock, whisky, and any juices from the steaks together in a bowl and pour into the skillet. Heat through, stirring, then pour over the steaks. Divide the carrots evenly among 4 warmed plates; add the steaks, garnish with a sprig of parsley, and serve immediately.

Spicy Pork Meatballs

INGREDIENTS

1 lb 8 oz/675 g fresh lean ground pork

1 garlic clove, finely chopped

1 tsp ground ginger

pinch of ground cloves

½ tsp freshly grated nutmeg

½ tsp ground allspice

½ tsp salt

½ tsp black pepper

2 egg yolks

¼ cup ground almonds

2–3 tbsp sunflower or olive oil

serves ❹

1 Preheat the broiler. Mix the ground pork, garlic, spices, salt, pepper, egg yolks, and ground almonds together in a large bowl. Form into balls and brush with the oil.

2 Broil the meatballs, turning from time to time for about 8 to 10 minutes, or until cooked through.

3 Alternatively, heat the oil in a large skillet and pan-fry the meatballs for about 8 to 10 minutes, or until cooked through. Serve immediately.

Ginger Pork

INGREDIENTS

2 tbsp sunflower or olive oil

½-inch/1-cm piece fresh ginger, peeled and grated

1 garlic clove, crushed

2 boneless pork steaks, cut into thin strips

3 oz/85 g shredded white cabbage

4 tbsp cashew nuts

2 tbsp dark soy sauce

1 tbsp dry white wine

1 tsp granulated sugar

1 tsp sesame oil

salt and pepper

serves ❷

1 Heat a wok over high heat and when smoking, add 1 tablespoon of oil, swirling it around the wok.

2 Add the ginger and garlic and cook quickly for 20 seconds. Add the pork and cook for 3 to 4 minutes, or until just cooked through. Remove the pork, ginger, and garlic from the wok and keep warm.

3 Add the remaining oil to the wok and when hot add the cabbage, and cook for 2 to 3 minutes until tender. Add the cashew nuts and cook for 3 seconds.

4 Return the pork, ginger, and garlic to the wok with the soy sauce, wine, and sugar. Cook for 1 minute then add the sesame oil and season with salt and pepper to taste.

Sweet & Sour Pork

INGREDIENTS

1 tbsp vegetable oil

12 oz/350 g lean pork, cut
into ¼-inch/5-mm strips

1 large bell pepper, seeded
and sliced

4 scallions, trimmed
and chopped

1 lb/450 g canned pineapple
pieces in juice

2 tbsp cornstarch

3 tbsp wine vinegar

juice of 1 lemon

3 tbsp light soy sauce

2 tbsp granulated sugar

salt and pepper

serves ❹

1 Heat the oil in a large skillet, add the pork strips, and cook for 5 minutes, stirring.

2 Add the bell pepper and scallions to the skillet and cook for 3 minutes, stirring until they begin to soften.

3 Drain the pineapple juice into a bowl, reserving the pineapple pieces, and whisk in the cornstarch, vinegar, lemon juice, soy sauce, sugar, and salt and pepper.

4 Add the mixture to the skillet and cook over medium heat for 1 to 2 minutes, stirring until slightly thickened. Add the reserved pineapple pieces and heat through for 1 minute. Serve immediately.

Florentine Ham

INGREDIENTS

good handful of fresh baby
spinach leaves

4 slices ham

salt and pepper

4 eggs

4 tbsp heavy cream

½ cup grated cheese, such as
Gruyère or cheddar

serves ❷

1 Preheat the broiler. Put the spinach in a large
bowl and pour boiling water over it. Let stand
until the leaves are wilted, then drain well on
paper towels.

2 Line 2 small ovenproof dishes with the ham,
it doesn't matter if the slices overlap the edges,
and spread the spinach evenly over the top.
Season well with salt and pepper.

3 Break in the eggs and drizzle over the cream.

4 Sprinkle with the cheese and broil for 8 to
10 minutes, or until the eggs are cooked to your
liking and the cheese is bubbling.

Venison Steaks in Red Currant Cream Sauce

INGREDIENTS

2 tbsp butter

1 tbsp vegetable oil

four 8 oz/225 g venison steaks

freshly cooked aparagus spears, to serve

FOR THE RED CURRANT CREAM SAUCE

2 tbsp water

2 tbsp red currant preserve

¾ cup heavy cream or sour cream

salt and pepper

serves ❹

1 Heat the butter and oil in a skillet and, when hot, add the venison steaks. Cook over high heat for 3 to 4 minutes on each side, depending on how rare you like your venison.

2 Remove the venison from the skillet and keep warm.

3 To make the sauce, add the water to the skillet and stir well. Add the red currant preserve and cream and bring to a boil. Season with salt and pepper to taste and spoon over the steaks. Serve immediately with freshly cooked asparagus spears.

2 Poultry

When cooking poultry there are a couple of shortcuts that can help you save time in the kitchen. Use cooked chicken or duck breasts for the recipes and reduce the cooking time accordingly. To speed up the cooking time of raw boneless chicken breasts, place them between two pieces of wax paper or plastic wrap and flatten them with a rolling pin.

Chicken Satay

INGREDIENTS

4 tbsp smooth peanut butter

heaping ⅓ cup soy sauce

4 skinless, boneless chicken breasts, cut into thin strips

TO SERVE

freshly cooked rice of your choice

lemon wedges

serves ❹

1 Preheat the broiler. Mix the peanut butter and soy sauce together in a bowl until smooth. Stir in the chicken strips, tossing well to coat in the mixture.

2 Thread the chicken strips onto 4 pre-soaked, wooden skewers and broil for about 5 minutes on each side until cooked through. Serve immediately with freshly cooked rice and lemon wedges.

Chicken with Creamy Penne

INGREDIENTS

7 oz/200 g fresh penne pasta

salt

1 tbsp olive oil

2 skinless, boneless chicken breasts

4 tbsp dry white wine

heaping 1 cup frozen peas

5 tbsp heavy cream

4–5 tbsp chopped fresh parsley, for sprinkling

serves ❷

1 Cook the penne in a large pan of boiling salted water for about 3 to 4 minutes, or according to the package directions, until tender but still firm to the bite.

2 Meanwhile, heat the oil in a skillet, add the chicken breasts, and cook over medium heat for about 4 minutes on each side.

3 Pour in the wine and cook over high heat until it has almost evaporated.

4 Drain the pasta. Add the peas, cream, and pasta to the chicken breasts in the skillet and stir well. Cover and simmer for 2 minutes. Serve immediately sprinkled with chopped parsley.

Stir-Fried Coconut Chicken

INGREDIENTS

2 tbsp vegetable oil

4 skinless, boneless chicken breasts, cut into strips

1 lemongrass stalk, finely shredded

heaping 1 cup slivered almonds

1¾ cups canned coconut milk

3 tbsp light soy sauce

3 tbsp chopped fresh cilantro

2–3 tbsp flaked coconut

serves ❹

1 Heat the oil in a wok and when almost smoking, add the chicken strips and stir-fry for 5 minutes until browned.

2 Add the lemongrass, almonds, coconut milk, and soy sauce. Bring to a boil then reduce the heat and simmer for 1 minute.

3 Serve immediately sprinkled with chopped cilantro and flaked coconut.

Fragrant Chicken

INGREDIENTS

1 fresh red chile, seeded and finely chopped

3 garlic cloves, finely chopped

4 scallions, trimmed and finely chopped

½–¾-inch/1–2-cm piece fresh ginger, peeled and cut into wafer thin slices

1 tsp ground coriander

1 tsp ground cumin

4 tbsp olive oil

4 tbsp pine nuts, lightly crushed

salt and pepper

4 skinless, boneless chicken breasts, cut into thin slices

1 tbsp chopped fresh cilantro

serves ❹

1 Combine the chile, garlic, scallions, ginger, ground coriander, cumin, 3 tablespoons of oil, and the pine nuts in a bowl and season with salt and pepper.

2 Heat the remaining oil in a wok and, when very hot, add the chicken slices. Cook over high heat for about 4 minutes, or until the chicken is browned on both sides.

3 Add the chile mixture and cook for 4 to 5 minutes, or until the chicken is completely cooked.

4 Stir in the fresh cilantro and serve immediately.

Chicken Nuggets with Barbecue Sauce

INGREDIENTS

4 tbsp dry breadcrumbs

2 tbsp grated Parmesan cheese

2 tsp chopped fresh thyme, or 1 tsp dried

1 tsp salt

pinch of black pepper

4 skinless, boneless chicken breasts, cut into cubes

8 tbsp melted butter

FOR THE BARBECUE SAUCE

4 tbsp butter

2 large onions, grated

1¼ cups cider vinegar or wine vinegar

1¼ cups tomato ketchup

scant 1 cup dark brown sugar

1–2 tsp Worcestershire sauce

salt and pepper

serves ❹

1 Preheat the oven to 400°F/200°C. Combine the breadcrumbs, cheese, thyme, and salt and pepper on a large flat plate or in a plastic food bag.

2 Toss the chicken cubes in the melted butter, then in the crumb mixture. Place on a baking sheet and bake in the oven for 10 minutes until crisp.

3 Meanwhile, make the sauce. Heat the butter in a pan, add the onions, and cook over low heat until soft but not browned.

4 Add the cider vinegar, tomato ketchup, sugar, Worcestershire sauce, and salt and pepper to taste and heat, stirring, until the sugar has dissolved completely. Bring to a boil then reduce the heat and simmer for 5 minutes.

5 Remove the chicken from the oven and serve with the sauce.

Chicken in Marsala Sauce

INGREDIENTS

2 tbsp all-purpose flour

salt and pepper

4 skinless, boneless chicken breasts, sliced lengthwise

3 tbsp olive oil

⅔ cup Marsala

2 bay leaves

1 tbsp butter

freshly cooked rice, to serve

serves ❹

1 Mix the flour, and salt and pepper together on a large plate or in a plastic food bag. Add the chicken and toss to coat.

2 Heat the oil in a skillet over medium heat. Add the chicken and cook for about 4 minutes on both sides until tender. Remove from the skillet and keep warm.

3 Skim most of the fat from the skillet and pour in the Marsala. Add the bay leaves and boil for 1 minute, stirring well, then add the butter with any juices from the chicken and cook until thickened.

4 Return the chicken to the skillet and heat through. Serve immediately with freshly cooked rice.

Turkey Steaks with Prosciutto & Sage

INGREDIENTS

2 skinless, boneless turkey steaks

salt and pepper

2 slices prosciutto, halved

4 fresh sage leaves

2 tbsp all-purpose flour

2 tbsp olive oil

1 tbsp butter

TO SERVE

freshly cooked red cabbage

lemon wedges

serves ❷

1 Slice each turkey steak in half horizontally into 2 thinner scallops.

2 Put each scallop between sheets of plastic wrap and pat out thinly without tearing. Season each scallop with salt and pepper.

3 Lay half a slice of ham on each scallop, put a sage leaf on top, and secure these with a toothpick.

4 Mix the flour, and salt and pepper together on a large plate and dust each scallop with the seasoned flour on both sides.

5 Heat the oil in a large skillet, add the butter, and wait until foaming. Add the scallops and pan-fry over high heat for 1½ minutes, sage-side down, then turn them over and pan-fry for an additional 30 seconds, or until golden brown and tender. Serve immediately with freshly cooked red cabbage and lemon wedges.

Duck Breasts with Citrus Glaze

INGREDIENTS

¼ cup light brown sugar, plus extra if needed

finely grated zest and juice of 1 orange

finely grated zest and juice of 1 large lemon

finely grated zest and juice of 1 lime

4 duck breasts, skin on

salt and pepper

2 tbsp olive oil

TO SERVE

sugar snap peas

orange wedges

serves ❹

1 Put the sugar in a small pan, add just enough water to cover, and heat gently until dissolved.

2 Add the zests and juices and bring to a boil. Reduce the heat and simmer for about 10 minutes until the zest is soft, and the liquid is syrupy. Remove the pan from the heat. Taste and add a little more sugar if necessary.

3 Meanwhile, score the skin of the duck breasts with a sharp knife in a criss-cross pattern and rub with salt and pepper.

4 Heat the oil in a skillet. Place the duck breasts skin-side up in the skillet and cook for 5 minutes on each side until the flesh is just pink. Keep warm.

5 Slice the duck breasts diagonally into 5–6 slices and arrange on warmed plates.

6 Arrange the sugar snap peas and orange wedges on each plate, spoon over the glaze, and serve immediately.

Asian Duck & Noodle Salad with Peanut Sauce

INGREDIENTS

2 carrots, peeled

2 celery stalks

1 cucumber

three 5 oz/140 g duck breasts

12 oz/350 g rice noodles, cooked according to directions on package, rinsed, and drained

FOR THE PEANUT SAUCE

2 garlic cloves, crushed

2 tbsp dark brown sugar

2 tbsp peanut butter

2 tbsp coconut cream

2 tbsp soy sauce

2 tbsp rice vinegar

2 tbsp sesame oil

½ tsp freshly ground black pepper

½ tsp Chinese five-spice powder

½ tsp ground ginger

serves ❸

1 Preheat the broiler. Cut the carrots, celery, and cucumber into thin strips and set aside.

2 Broil the duck breasts for about 5 minutes on each side until cooked through. Let cool.

3 Meanwhile, heat all the ingredients for the sauce in a small pan until combined and the sugar has dissolved completely. Stir until smooth.

4 Slice the duck breasts. Divide the noodles among 3 serving bowls. Place the reserved carrots, celery, and cucumber on top of the noodles, arrange the duck slices on top, and drizzle with the sauce. Serve immediately.

Honeyed Duck Stir-Fry

INGREDIENTS

2 tbsp honey

4 tbsp soy sauce

4 skinless duck breasts, sliced

1 tbsp olive oil

bunch of scallions, trimmed and sliced

1 small head Chinese cabbage, finely shredded

salt and pepper

serves **4**

1 Mix the honey and soy sauce together in a large bowl. Add the duck slices and toss to coat in the mixture.

2 Heat the oil in a wok or skillet. Add the duck strips (set aside the honey mixture) and cook quickly for 2 minutes until browned.

3 Add the scallions, Chinese cabbage, and the reserved honey mixture. Cook for 3 to 4 minutes until the duck is cooked but still a little pink in the center.

4 Season with salt and pepper and serve immediately.

3 Seafood

There's nothing tastier than sparklingly fresh fish simply cooked. If you're skinning fish yourself, dip your fingers in salt beforehand to give a better grip and faster results. A tip for coating fish is to mix the ingredients for coating the fish in a plastic food bag, add the fish, and shake gently until coated.

Garlic-Sizzled Shrimp with Chili Dipping Sauce

INGREDIENTS

2 tbsp sunflower or olive oil

1–2 garlic cloves, crushed

bunch of scallions, trimmed and chopped

12 oz/350 g raw shrimp

chopped fresh chives or cilantro, to garnish

lime wedges, to serve

FOR THE CHILI DIPPING SAUCE

2 tbsp molasses

6 tbsp white wine vinegar

2 tbsp Thai fish sauce or light soy sauce

2 tbsp water

1 garlic clove, crushed

2 tsp grated fresh ginger

2 tsp finely chopped, seeded fresh red chile

serves ❸ to ❹

1 To make the sauce, heat the molasses, vinegar, fish sauce, and water in a small pan until boiling. Add the garlic, ginger, and chile and pour into a small serving bowl.

2 Heat the oil in a wok or skillet and add the garlic and scallions. Cook over high heat for 2 minutes then add the shrimp, stir-frying them for an additional 2 to 3 minutes.

3 Divide among 4 warmed serving plates, garnish with chives, and serve with the chili dipping sauce and lime wedges.

Wine-Steamed Mussels

INGREDIENTS

8 tbsp butter

1 shallot, chopped

3 garlic cloves, finely chopped

4½ lb/2 kg live mussels, scrubbed and beards removed (discard any open mussels or any that don't close immediately when sharply tapped)

1 cup dry white wine

½ tsp salt

pepper

4 tbsp chopped fresh parsley

serves ❹

1 Melt half the butter in a very large pan over low heat. Add the shallot and garlic and cook for 2 minutes. Add the mussels, wine, salt, and a sprinkling of pepper.

2 Cover, bring to a boil, then boil for 3 minutes, shaking the pan from time to time.

3 Remove the mussels from the pan with a slotted spoon and place in individual serving bowls. Discard any mussels that haven't opened.

4 Mix the remaining butter with the parsley in a small bowl and stir the mixture into the cooking juices in the pan. Bring to a boil and pour over the mussels. Serve immediately.

Oysters au Gratin

INGREDIENTS

4 oz/115 g pancetta or bacon, diced

1 oz/25 g celery, finely chopped

4 asparagus tips, finely chopped

salt and pepper

6 fresh oysters, shucked

1 oz/25 g firm mozzarella cheese, grated

serves ❷

1 Preheat the broiler. Cook the pancetta in a small skillet for 1 to 2 minutes until crisp. Add the celery and asparagus and season with salt and pepper to taste.

2 Spoon the pancetta and asparagus mixture over the oysters. Sprinkle over the grated cheese.

3 Cook the oysters under a medium-hot broiler for 3 to 4 minutes, or until the cheese is golden brown and melted. Serve immediately.

Pancetta-Wrapped Scallops

INGREDIENTS

16 large fresh scallops

8 slices pancetta, halved

1 tbsp olive oil

juice of 1 lemon

pepper

lemon wedges, to serve

serves ❹

1 Preheat the broiler. Wrap each scallop in half a slice of pancetta.

2 Mix the oil, lemon juice, and a sprinkling of black pepper together in a bowl.

3 Coat the wrapped scallops in the mixture and thread onto metal skewers (4 on each skewer). Discard any leftover lemon juice mixture.

4 Cook the wrapped scallops under a medium-hot broiler for 4 to 5 minutes, turning once until cooked. Serve immediatey, with the lemon wedges.

Poached Scallops with Sweet Dill Dressing

INGREDIENTS

12 fresh queen scallops with their corals

finely grated zest and juice of 2 limes

⅔ cup dry white wine

bunch of scallions, trimmed and sliced diagonally

salt and pepper

2 tbsp granulated sugar

4 tbsp butter

2 tbsp chopped fresh dill

FOR GARNISH

fresh dill sprigs

lime slices

serves 4

1 Put the scallops in a shallow dish. Mix the lime zest, juice, wine, scallions, salt and pepper, and sugar together in a bowl. Pour the mixture over the scallops and turn them to coat well.

2 Heat the butter in a skillet. Using a slotted spoon, remove the scallops from the lime mixture and add to the skillet. Set aside the lime juice mixture. Pan-fry for 2 minutes on each side until almost tender.

3 Stir the lime juice mixture and chopped dill into the skillet. Bring to a boil and boil rapidly for 8 minutes until reduced.

4 Serve immediately, garnished with dill sprigs and lime slices.

Hot & Sour Shrimp Soup

INGREDIENTS

10½ oz/300 g raw peeled shrimp

2 tsp vegetable oil

2 fresh red chiles, sliced

1 garlic clove, sliced

about 3 cups fish stock

4 thin slices fresh ginger

2 lemongrass stalks, bruised

5 Thai lime leaves, shredded

2 tsp jaggery or brown sugar

1 tbsp chili oil

handful of fresh cilantro leaves

dash of lime juice

serves ❷

1 Dry-fry the shrimp in a skillet or wok until they turn pink. Remove and set aside.

2 Heat the vegetable oil in the same skillet, add the chiles and garlic and cook for 30 seconds.

3 Add the stock, ginger, lemongrass, Thai lime leaves, and sugar and simmer for 4 minutes. Add the reserved shrimp with the chili oil, and cilantro and cook for 1 to 2 minutes.

4 Stir in the lime juice and serve immediately.

Smoked Salmon Pâté

INGREDIENTS

1 lb/450 g smoked salmon, chopped into small pieces

1 tsp chopped fresh thyme

juice and finely grated zest of 1 small lemon

2 tbsp soft unsalted butter

⅓ cup soft cream cheese

pinch of paprika

pinch of cayenne pepper

pepper

crispbreads, to serve

makes about 1 lb/450 g

1 Put the smoked salmon, thyme, lemon juice, and zest in a food processor and process until just combined.

2 Scrape down the sides of the bowl, and add the butter and cheese. Season lightly with the paprika, cayenne, and pepper.

3 Process again until the mixture is blended, but not completely smooth—it should still have a slightly rough texture. Taste and adjust the seasoning, if necessary.

4 Transfer to an airtight container. Cover and let chill in the refrigerator until firm. Remove from the refrigerator at least 15 minutes before eating and serve with crispbreads.

Seared Salmon with Cannellini Bean Mash

INGREDIENTS

four 6 oz/175 g salmon steaks

finely grated zest and juice
of 1 lemon

3 tbsp maple syrup

1 tbsp wholegrain mustard

½ tsp salt

FOR THE CANNELLINI BEAN MASH

three 14 oz/400 g cans
cannellini beans, drained

1 tbsp olive oil

5 tbsp sour cream

1 garlic clove, crushed

salt and pepper

serves ❹

1 Preheat the broiler. Lay the salmon steaks in an ovenproof dish.

2 Mix the lemon zest and juice, maple syrup, mustard, and ½ teaspoon of salt together in a bowl. Pour over the salmon and broil without turning for about 6 minutes until the salmon is cooked through.

3 For the mash, heat the beans, oil, sour cream, and garlic in a pan until bubbling. Season with plenty of salt and pepper and mash with a wooden spoon.

4 Place the salmon alongside the mashed beans and pour over the cooking juices.

Peppered Tuna Steaks

INGREDIENTS

four 6 oz/175 g tuna steaks

4 tsp sunflower or olive oil

1 tsp salt

2 tbsp pink, green, and black peppercorns, coarsely crushed

FOR SERVING

4 baked potatoes (optional)

2 tbsp butter (optional)

handful of fresh arugula leaves

lemon wedges

serves 4

1 Brush the tuna steaks with the oil and sprinkle with salt.

2 Coat the tuna in the crushed peppercorns.

3 Meanwhile, heat a ridged grill pan or skillet and, when hot, add the fish and cook over medium heat for 2 to 3 minutes on each side. Serve with baked potatoes, if using, dabbed with a little butter, some arugula leaves, and the lemon wedges on the side.

Fish Goujons with Chili Mayonnaise

INGREDIENTS

scant 1½ cups all-purpose flour

salt and pepper

3 eggs

heaping 1 cup matzo meal

1 lb/450 g firm white fish, such as monkfish, cut into strips

sunflower or peanut oil, for frying

FOR THE CHILI MAYONNAISE

2 tbsp sweet chili sauce

4–5 tbsp mayonnaise

serves ❹

1 Mix the flour with plenty of salt and pepper on a large flat plate. Beat the eggs in a bowl and spread the matzo meal out on another flat plate.

2 Dip the fish pieces into the seasoned flour, then into the beaten egg, then into the matzo meal, ensuring a generous coating.

3 Pour the oil into a nonstick or heavy-bottom skillet to give a depth of ½ inch/1 cm, and then heat it up. Cook the fish pieces in batches for a few minutes, turning once, until golden and cooked through.

4 To make the chili mayonnaise, beat the chili sauce and mayonnaise together in a bowl until combined.

5 Transfer the fish to warmed plates and serve with the chili mayonnaise on the side.

Lemon & Parsley Crusted Monkfish

INGREDIENTS

4 tbsp sunflower oil
or melted butter

4 tbsp fresh breadcrumbs

4 tbsp chopped fresh parsley

finely grated zest of 1 large
lemon

salt and pepper

4 monkfish fillets, about
5–6 oz/140–175 g

fresh sprigs of parsley, to
garnish

4 potatoes, peeled, diced,
and deep-fried, to serve
(optional)

serves ❹

1 Preheat the oven to 350°F/180°C. Mix the oil, breadcrumbs, parsley, and lemon zest with a sprinkling of salt and pepper together in a bowl to give a smooth mixture.

2 Place the fish fillets on a large roasting tray. Divide the breadcrumb mixture between them and press it down onto the fish with your fingers to ensure it covers the fillets.

3 Bake in the oven for 7 to 8 minutes, or until the fish is cooked. Garnish with fresh sprigs of parsley, and serve with deep-fried potato cubes, if desired.

Seafood Kabobs

INGREDIENTS

1 lb/450 g skinless, boneless fish, such as monkfish, swordfish, and halibut

1 lemon, cut into 8 wedges

8 bay leaves

3 tbsp olive oil

serves 2 to 4

1 Preheat the broiler. Cut the fish into cubes and thread onto 4 pre-soaked, wooden skewers, alternating with the lemon and bay leaves.

2 Brush with oil and cook under medium-hot broiler for about 4 minutes on each side until the fish is cooked. Serve.

Microwave Herbed Fish Parcels

INGREDIENTS

four 4 oz/115 g firm white fish
fillets, such as monkfish

4 tbsp lemon juice

4 tbsp white wine or cider

4 tbsp chopped fresh parsley

4 fresh thyme sprigs

4 fresh rosemary sprigs

4 tomatoes, thinly sliced

serves 4

1 Place a fish fillet in the center of four
12-inch/30-cm squares of parchment paper.

2 Sprinkle each fillet with 1 tablespoon of
lemon juice and 1 tablespoon of white wine,
followed by 1 tablespoon of chopped parsley.
Add a sprig of thyme and rosemary
to each parcel.

3 Arrange the sliced tomatoes over each fillet,
overlapping them. Fold in the edges of the
parchment paper squares to completely
enclose the filling and form parcels. Place the
parcels in a circle on a heatproof plate, leaving
a 1-inch/2.5-cm space between each parcel,
and cook in the microwave oven on HIGH for
7 minutes. Serve immediately.

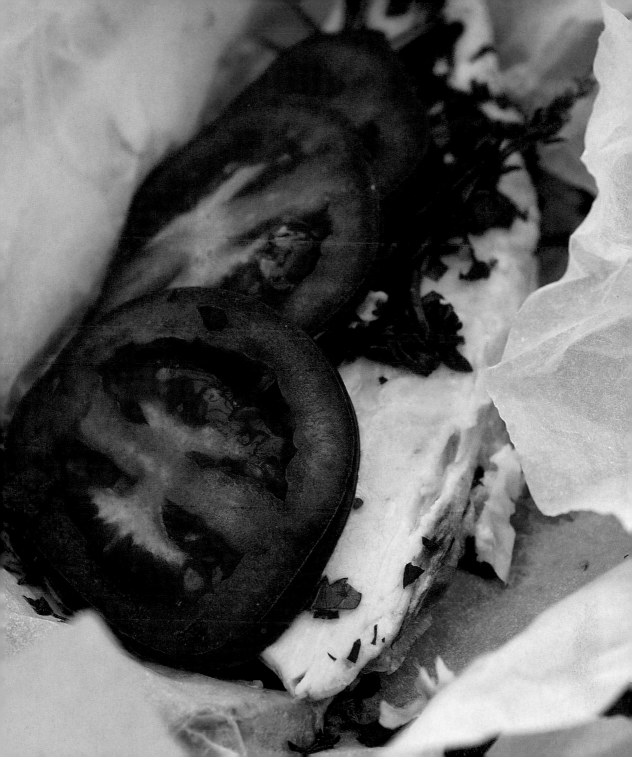

Spicy Tuna Fishcakes

INGREDIENTS

4 tbsp all-purpose flour

salt and pepper

7 oz/200 g canned tuna in oil, drained

2–3 tbsp curry paste

1 scallion, trimmed and finely chopped

1 egg, beaten

sunflower or peanut oil, for frying

arugula leaves, to serve

makes **4** fishcakes

1 Mix the flour with plenty of salt and pepper on a large flat plate. Mash the tuna with the curry paste, scallion, and beaten egg in a large bowl.

2 Form into 4 patties and dust in the seasoned flour.

3 Heat the oil in a skillet, add the patties, and fry for 3 to 4 minutes on each side until crisp and golden. Serve on a bed of arugula leaves.

4 Egg & Cheese

Eggs must be the original fast food because they take just minutes to cook. Cheese adds flavor and texture to all sorts of dishes, and you can change the flavor of any of these recipes by using different varieties of cheese. Always keep some eggs and cheese in the refrigerator and you'll never be stuck for a tasty meal!

Spiced Scrambled Eggs

INGREDIENTS

4 eggs

⅔ cup light cream

salt and pepper

pinch of saffron

2 tbsp butter

½ tsp ground cumin

½–1 tsp harissa paste

1 tsp ground coriander

2 slices of freshly toasted bread, buttered if desired, to serve

serves ❷

1 Whisk the eggs, cream, salt and pepper, and saffron together in a bowl.

2 Melt the butter in a skillet and add the cumin, harissa, and ground coriander. Cook gently for 1 minute.

3 Pour in the egg mixture and cook, stirring, for a few minutes until the eggs are just set. Serve the spiced scrambled eggs on top of the freshly toasted bread.

Provençal Frittata

INGREDIENTS

3 tbsp sunflower or olive oil

1 garlic clove, chopped

8 oz/225 g fresh or frozen spinach

salt and pepper

handful of cherry tomatoes, halved

6 eggs, whisked

cherry tomatoes on the vine, to serve (optional)

serves ❷ to ❹

1 Heat the oil in a large skillet, add the garlic, and cook for 1 minute then add the spinach and cook for an additional 1 minute until wilted.

2 Season with salt and pepper, add the cherry tomatoes to the skillet, and cook for 1 minute.

3 Pour the eggs into the skillet, stirring, and cook for 4 to 5 minutes until set. Serve hot or cold cut into wedges, with cherry tomatoes on the vine, if using.

Egg & Bacon Salad

INGREDIENTS

1 tbsp sunflower or olive oil

6–8 slices bacon, diced

1 cup fresh breadcrumbs

selection of salad greens, torn

6–8 hard-cooked eggs, quartered

12 black olives

FOR THE DRESSING

2 tbsp white wine vinegar

5 tbsp extra virgin olive oil

1 tbsp whole grain mustard

salt and pepper

serves ❹

1 Heat the sunflower or olive oil in a skillet, add the bacon, and cook for about 5 minutes until crisp. Remove from the skillet.

2 Add the breadcrumbs to the skillet and cook over high heat until crisp and golden. Set aside.

3 Put the salad greens into a bowl with the eggs and olives and tip in the bacon.

4 For the dressing, whisk the vinegar, extra virgin olive oil, mustard, and salt and pepper together in a bowl and pour over the salad.

5 Toss to mix, sprinkle with the crisp breadcrumbs, and serve immediately.

Spaghetti Carbonara

INGREDIENTS

1 lb/450 g fresh spaghetti

2 tbsp butter

6 slices bacon, diced

3 eggs

2 tbsp light cream

4 tbsp freshly grated
Parmesan cheese

salt and pepper

fresh parsley, chopped,
for sprinkling

serves ❹

1 Cook the spaghetti in a large pan of boiling salted water for about 2 to 4 minutes, or according to the package directions, until tender but still firm to the bite.

2 Meanwhile, heat the butter in a skillet, add the bacon, and cook until crisp. Keep warm.

3 Beat the eggs, cream, and cheese together in a bowl and season with salt and pepper.

4 As soon as the spaghetti is cooked, drain and return to the pan over low heat.

5 Add the bacon, and egg and cream mixture, and quickly toss the spaghetti several times until the sauce begins to thicken and the spaghetti is coated. Serve immediately sprinkled with chopped parsley.

Goat Cheese Tarts

INGREDIENTS

butter, for greasing

14 oz/400 g package prepared and rolled puff pastry

1 tbsp all-purpose flour

1 egg, beaten

3 tbsp onion relish or tomato relish

three 4 oz/115 g goat cheese logs, sliced

olive oil, for drizzling

pepper

makes about 12 tarts

1 Preheat the oven to 400°F/200°C and grease several baking sheets.

2 Cut out as many 3-inch/7.5-cm circles as possible from the pastry on a lightly floured counter.

3 Place the circles on the baking sheets and press gently, about 1 inch/2.5 cm from the edge of each, with a smaller 2-inch/5-cm dough cutter.

4 Brush the circles with beaten egg and prick with a fork.

5 Top each circle with a little relish and a slice of goat cheese. Drizzle with oil and sprinkle over a little black pepper.

6 Bake for 8 to 10 minutes, or until the pastry is crisp and the cheese is bubbling. Serve warm.

Warm Goat Cheese Salad

INGREDIENTS

1 small iceberg lettuce, torn
into pieces

handful of arugula leaves

few radicchio leaves, torn

6 slices French bread

4 oz/115 g goat cheese, sliced

FOR THE DRESSING

4 tbsp extra virgin olive oil

1 tbsp white wine vinegar

salt and pepper

serves ❹

1 Preheat the broiler. Divide all the leaves among 4 individual salad bowls.

2 Toast one side of the bread under the broiler until golden. Place a slice of cheese on top of each untoasted side and toast until the cheese is just melting.

3 Put all the dressing ingredients into a bowl and beat together until combined. Pour over the leaves, tossing to coat.

4 Cut each slice of bread in half and place 3 halves on top of each salad. Toss very gently to combine and serve warm.

Pizza Express

INGREDIENTS

9-inch/23-cm ready-made pizza base

fresh basil leaves, torn

FOR THE TOMATO TOPPING

2/3 cup crushed tomatoes

3 tbsp tomato paste

2 garlic cloves, crushed

pinch each of sugar, salt, and pepper

handful of cherry tomatoes

FOR THE CHEESE TOPPING

2/3 cup crushed tomatoes

3 tbsp tomato paste

4 oz/115 g jar roasted peppers, drained and thickly sliced

a few black olives

salt and pepper

4 oz/115 g firm mozzarella cheese, grated

2 oz/55 g Parmesan cheese, grated

serves 4 to 6

1 Preheat the oven to 400°F/200°C. To make the tomato topping, mix the crushed tomatoes, tomato paste, garlic, sugar, and salt and pepper together in a bowl. Spread over the ready-made pizza base and scatter with the cherry tomatoes.

2 To make the cheese topping, mix the crushed tomatoes and tomato paste together in a bowl and spread over the pizza base. Top with the peppers and the olives. Season with salt and pepper and scatter the mozzarella and Parmesan cheeses over the top.

3 Bake in the oven for 8 to 10 minutes until hot and bubbling. Scatter with basil leaves and serve immediately.

Creamy Ricotta, Mint & Garlic Pasta

INGREDIENTS

serves ❹

10½ oz/300 g short fresh pasta shapes

salt and pepper

heaping ½ cup ricotta cheese

1–2 roasted garlic cloves from a jar, finely chopped

⅔ cup heavy cream

1 tbsp chopped fresh mint, and 4 sprigs to garnish

1 Cook the pasta in a large pan of boiling salted water for about 3 minutes, or according to the package directions until tender but still firm to the bite.

2 Beat the ricotta, garlic, cream, and chopped mint together in a bowl until smooth.

3 Drain the cooked pasta then tip back into the pan. Pour in the cheese mixture and toss together.

4 Season with pepper and serve immediately, garnished with the sprigs of mint.

Baked Chili Cheese Sandwiches

INGREDIENTS

3½ cups grated cheese, such as cheddar

8 tbsp butter, softened, plus extra to finish

4 fresh green chiles, seeded and chopped

½ tsp ground cumin

8 thick slices bread

makes ❹ sandwiches

1 Preheat the oven to 375°F/190°C. Mix the cheese and butter together in a bowl until creamy then add the chiles and cumin.

2 Spread this mixture over 4 slices of bread and top with the remaining slices.

3 Spread the outside of the sandwiches with extra butter and bake for 8 to 10 minutes until crisp. Serve.

Caramel-Topped Brie

INGREDIENTS

2 tbsp water

scant 1 cup granulated sugar

1 whole mini Brie cheese

FOR SERVING (OPTIONAL)

8 oatcakes

4 handfuls fresh, washed white grapes

serves ❹

1 Heat the water and sugar in a pan over low heat until the sugar has dissolved completely.

2 Increase the heat and cook steadily until the sugar is a dark golden color.

3 Remove the pan from the heat then immediately pour over the Brie and let set. Serve at room temperature and crack the caramel before serving, with oatcakes and fresh grapes, if using.

Broiled Provolone with Herbed Couscous

INGREDIENTS

1 lb/450 g provolone cheese, cut into ¼-inch/5-mm slices

4 tbsp chili oil

FOR THE HERBED COUSCOUS

1¾ cups hot vegetable stock

heaping 1 cup couscous

2 tbsp chopped fresh mixed herbs

2 tsp lemon juice

1 tbsp olive oil

serves ❹

1 Preheat the broiler to high and line the broiler rack with foil.

2 Put the cheese slices in a bowl, pour over the chili oil, and toss well to coat the cheese.

3 Place the cheese on the broiler rack and cook under the broiler for 2 to 3 minutes on each side until golden.

4 Meanwhile, stir the hot stock into the couscous in a large bowl. Cover and let stand for 5 minutes.

5 Stir the herbs, lemon juice, and olive oil into the couscous and serve with the broiled provolone cheese.

Mozzarella Gnocchi

INGREDIENTS

butter, for greasing

1 lb/450 g package potato gnocchi

scant 1 cup heavy cream

8 oz/225 g firm mozzarella cheese, grated or chopped

salt and pepper

serves 2 to 4

1 Preheat the broiler and grease a large baking dish.

2 Cook the gnocchi in a large pan of boiling salted water for about 3 minutes, or according to the package directions.

3 Drain and put into the prepared baking dish.

4 Season the cream with salt and pepper and drizzle over the gnocchi. Scatter over the cheese and cook under the broiler for a few minutes until the top is browned and bubbling. Serve immediately.

5 Vegetarian

Colorful tasty vegetables with clear well-defined flavors are delicious in their own right. Adding different herbs to recipes, such as a sprinkling of chopped mint to a pea soup recipe, will completely alter the flavor. A handful of chopped toasted nuts or crumbled cheese will also add interest and color to plain salads.

Chilled Avocado Soup

INGREDIENTS

4 ripe avocados, peeled

1 garlic clove

5 cups vegetable stock

4 tbsp lime juice

pinch of cayenne pepper

salt and pepper

2 tbsp chives, snipped,
to garnish

French bread, to serve

serves ❻

1 Put the avocados, garlic, stock, lime juice, and cayenne into a food processor or blender and process until smooth.

2 Season with salt and pepper to taste and let chill in the refrigerator until ready to serve with French bread and garnished with snipped chives.

Garden Pea Soup

INGREDIENTS

2½ cups vegetable stock

1 lb/450 g fresh peas

salt and pepper

pinch of granulated sugar

½ cup light cream

FOR SERVING

2 tbsp light cream

4 crusty rolls

serves ❹

1 Bring the stock to a boil in a large pan. Add the peas and cook for 5 minutes.

2 Remove the pan from the heat, season with salt, pepper, and sugar, then transfer to a food processor and process until smooth.

3 Pour into a pan, stir in the cream, and heat gently to simmering point.

4 Taste and adjust the seasoning if necessary, then pour into 4 serving bowls, adding a swirl of light cream to each bowl and serving with crusty rolls.

Quesadillas

INGREDIENTS

4 tbsp finely chopped fresh jalapeño chiles

1 onion, chopped

1 tbsp red wine vinegar

5 tbsp extra virgin olive oil

10½–14 oz/300–400 g canned corn

8 soft flour tortillas

serves ❹

1 Put the chiles, onion, vinegar, and 4 tablespoons of olive oil in a food processor and process until finely chopped.

2 Tip into a bowl and stir in the corn.

3 Heat the remaining oil in a skillet, add a tortilla, and cook for 1 minute until golden.

4 Spread the chili mixture over the tortilla and fold over.

5 Cook for 2 to 3 minutes until golden and the filling is heated through. Remove from the skillet and keep warm. Repeat with the other tortillas and filling. Serve immediately.

Creamed Mushrooms

INGREDIENTS

juice of 1 small lemon

1 lb/450 g small button mushrooms

2 tbsp butter

1 tbsp sunflower or olive oil

1 small onion, finely chopped

salt and pepper

½ cup whipping or heavy cream

1 tbsp chopped fresh parsley, plus 4 sprigs to garnish

serves ❹

1 Sprinkle a little of the lemon juice over the mushrooms.

2 Heat the butter and oil in a skillet, add the onion, and cook for 1 minute. Add the mushrooms, shaking the skillet so they do not stick.

3 Season with salt and pepper to taste, then stir in the cream, chopped parsley, and remaining lemon juice.

4 Heat until hot but don't let boil then transfer to a serving plate and garnish with the parsley sprigs. Serve immediately.

Tofu Stir-Fry

INGREDIENTS

2 tbsp sunflower or olive oil

12 oz/350 g firm tofu, cubed

8 oz/225 g bok choy, coarsely chopped

1 garlic clove, chopped

4 tbsp sweet chili sauce

2 tbsp light soy sauce

serves ❹

1 Heat 1 tablespoon of oil in a wok, add the tofu in batches, and stir-fry for 2 to 3 minutes until golden. Remove and set aside.

2 Add the bok choy to the wok and stir-fry for a few seconds until tender and wilted. Remove and set aside.

3 Add the remaining oil to the wok, then add the garlic and stir-fry for 30 seconds.

4 Stir in the chili sauce and soy sauce and bring to a boil.

5 Return the tofu and bok choy to the wok and toss gently until coated in the sauce. Serve immediately.

Noodle Stir-Fry

INGREDIENTS

5 oz/140 g flat rice noodles

6 tbsp soy sauce

2 tbsp lemon juice

1 tsp granulated sugar

½ tsp cornstarch

1 tbsp vegetable oil

2 tsp grated fresh ginger

2 garlic cloves, chopped

4–5 scallions, trimmed and sliced

2 tbsp rice wine or dry sherry

7 oz/200 g canned water chestnuts, sliced

serves ❷

1 Put the noodles in a large bowl and cover with boiling water. Let stand for 4 minutes. Drain and rinse under cold running water.

2 Mix the soy sauce, lemon juice, sugar, and cornstarch together in small bowl.

3 Heat the oil in a wok, add the ginger and garlic, and stir-fry for 1 minute.

4 Add the scallions and stir-fry for 3 minutes.

5 Add the rice wine or dry sherry, followed by the soy sauce mixture and cook for 1 minute.

6 Stir in the water chestnuts and noodles and cook for an additional 1 to 2 minutes, or until heated through. Serve immediately.

Falafel Burgers

INGREDIENTS

serves ❹

two 14 oz/400 g can chickpeas, drained and rinsed

1 small onion, chopped

zest and juice of 1 lime

2 tsp ground coriander

2 tsp ground cumin

6 tbsp all-purpose flour

4 tbsp olive oil

4 fresh basil sprigs, to garnish

tomato salsa, to serve

1 Put the chickpeas, onion, lime zest and juice, and the spices into a food processor and process to a coarse paste.

2 Tip the mixture out onto a clean counter or cutting board and shape into 4 patties.

3 Spread the flour out on a large flat plate and use to coat the patties.

4 Heat the oil in a large skillet, add the burgers, and cook for 2 minutes on each side until crisp. Garnish with basil and serve with tomato salsa.

Tagliatelle with Lemon & Thyme

INGREDIENTS

12 oz/350 g fresh tagliatelle

6 tbsp butter

finely grated zest and juice of 1 lemon

2 tbsp chopped fresh thyme

salt and pepper

serves ❷ to ❹

1 Cook the pasta in a large pan of boiling salted water for about 4 minutes, or according to the package directions until tender but still firm to the bite.

2 Drain the pasta, keeping about 3 tablespoons of the cooking liquid in it. Stir in the butter, grated lemon zest and lemon juice, thyme, and salt and pepper, and toss well to mix. Serve immediately.

Pasta with Spicy Olive Sauce

INGREDIENTS

12 oz/350 g fresh pasta shapes

salt

6 tbsp olive oil

½ tsp freshly grated nutmeg

½ tsp black pepper

1 garlic clove, crushed

2 tbsp tapenade

½ cup black or green olives, pitted and sliced

1 tbsp chopped fresh parsley, to garnish (optional)

serves ❷ to ❹

1 Cook the pasta in a large pan of boiling salted water for about 4 minutes, or according to the package directions until tender but still firm to the bite.

2 Meanwhile, put ½ teaspoon of salt with the oil, nutmeg, pepper, garlic, tapenade, and olives in another saucepan and heat slowly but do not allow to boil. Cover and let stand for 3 to 4 minutes.

3 Drain the pasta and return to the pan. Add the flavored oil and heat gently for 1 to 2 minutes. Serve immediately, garnished with chopped parsley, if using.

Chinese-Style Gingered Vegetables

INGREDIENTS

1 tbsp sunflower or peanut oil

1-inch/2.5-cm piece fresh ginger, peeled and grated

1 onion, thinly sliced

4 oz/115 g frozen green string beans, cut into small pieces

1 lb/450 g bag frozen mixed vegetables

²/₃ cup water

2 heaping tbsp dark brown sugar

2 tbsp cornstarch

4 tbsp vinegar

4 tbsp soy sauce

1 tsp ground ginger

serves ❷

1 Heat the oil in a wok or large skillet, add the grated ginger, and sauté for 1 minute. Remove from the wok or skillet and drain on paper towels.

2 Reduce the heat slightly and add the vegetables and water to the wok.

3 Cover with a lid or foil and cook for 5 to 6 minutes, or until the vegetables are tender.

4 Mix the sugar, cornstarch, vinegar, soy sauce, and ground ginger together in a bowl. Increase the heat to medium and add the mixture to the vegetables in the wok. Simmer for 1 minute, stirring, until thickened.

5 Return the ginger to the wok and stir to mix well. Heat through for 2 minutes and then serve immediately.

Vegetable Tartlets

INGREDIENTS

butter, for greasing

12 ready-baked pastry shells

2 tbsp olive oil

1 red bell pepper, seeded and diced

1 garlic clove, crushed

1 small onion, finely chopped

8 oz/225 g ripe tomatoes, chopped

1 tbsp torn fresh basil

1 tsp fresh or dried thyme

salt and pepper

green salad, to serve

makes ⑫ tartlets

1 Preheat the oven to 400°F/200°C and grease several baking sheets.

2 Place the ready-baked pastry shells on the prepared baking sheets.

3 Heat the oil in a skillet, add the bell pepper, garlic, and onion, and cook over high heat for about 3 minutes until soft.

4 Add the tomatoes, herbs, and seasoning and spoon onto the pastry shells.

5 Bake for about 5 minutes, or until the filling is piping hot. Serve warm with a green salad.

Wilted Spinach, Yogurt & Walnut Salad

INGREDIENTS

1 lb/450 g fresh spinach leaves

1 onion, chopped

1 tbsp olive oil

salt and pepper

1 cup plain yogurt

1 garlic clove, finely chopped

2 tbsp chopped toasted walnuts

2–3 tsp chopped fresh mint

pita bread, to serve

serves ❷

1 Put the spinach and onion into a pan, cover, and cook gently for a few minutes until the spinach has wilted.

2 Add the oil and cook for an additional 5 minutes. Season with salt and pepper to taste.

3 Combine the yogurt and garlic in a bowl.

4 Put the spinach and onion into a serving bowl and pour over the yogurt mixture. Scatter over the walnuts and chopped mint and serve with pita bread.

Moroccan Carrot & Orange Salad

INGREDIENTS

1 lb/450 g carrots, peeled

1 tbsp olive oil

2 tbsp lemon juice

pinch of granulated sugar

2 large oranges, peeled and cut into segments (reserve any juice)

⅓ cup raisins

1 tsp ground cinnamon

2 tbsp toasted pine nuts

serves ❹

1 Grate the carrots into a large bowl.

2 In a separate bowl, combine the oil, lemon juice, sugar, and any orange juice reserved from the preparing of the orange segments.

3 Toss the orange segments with the carrots and stir in the raisins and cinnamon.

4 Pour over the dressing and scatter over the pine nuts just before serving.

Hot Tomato & Basil Salad

INGREDIENTS

serves **6**

1½ lb/700 g cherry tomatoes

1 garlic clove, crushed

2 tbsp capers, drained and rinsed

1 tsp granulated sugar

4 tbsp olive oil

2 tbsp torn fresh basil

1 Preheat the oven to 400°F/200°C. Stir the tomatoes, garlic, capers, and sugar together in a bowl and tip into a roasting pan.

2 Pour over the oil and toss to coat.

3 Cook in the oven for 10 minutes until the tomatoes are hot.

4 Remove from the oven and tip into a heatproof serving bowl. Scatter over the basil and serve immediately.

6 Fruit

Fresh fruit is one of the healthiest and most delicious ways to end a meal. Make an unusual fruit salad with a variety of seasonal fruits steeped in lemonade or ginger beer. A quick snack that children love is bananas coated in melted chocolate (milk, semisweet, or white) and rolled in dry, unsweetened coconut or chopped nuts.

Pan-Fried Pears with Maple Syrup & Walnuts

INGREDIENTS

6 tbsp butter

4 firm pears or apples, cut into thick slices

3 tbsp maple syrup

2 tbsp brandy

4 tbsp walnuts

serves ❹

1 Melt half the butter in a skillet and add half the pears or apples.

2 Cook for 2 minutes on each side until golden. Remove from the skillet and cook the remaining fruit, then remove from the skillet.

3 Add the remaining butter to the skillet with the maple syrup, brandy, and walnuts and bring to a boil. Remove from the heat.

4 Put the warm fruit into serving bowls and pour over the sauce. Serve.

Strawberry & Banana Cream

INGREDIENTS

4 large bananas

1 lb/450 g strawberries, hulled, plus extra whole strawberries, to decorate

1¼ cups heavy cream, whipped

granulated or superfine sugar, if necessary

cookies, such as cigarette russe, to serve

serves ❹ to ❻

1 Peel the bananas and put in a food processor with the strawberries. Process to a purée and tip into a large bowl.

2 Gently stir in the whipped cream. Sweeten to taste if needed.

3 Chill in the refrigerator until ready to serve with cookies and decorated with a strawberry.

Berry Brûlées

INGREDIENTS

1 lb/450 g berries, such as raspberries, strawberries, red currants, and pitted cherries

1¼ cups heavy cream

½ cup superfine sugar

serves 4 to 6

1 Preheat the broiler to very hot. Divide the berries into 4–6 individual ovenproof dishes or one large dish.

2 Whip the cream in a large bowl until thick but not stiff.

3 Spoon the cream over the berries until they are evenly covered.

4 Sprinkle over the sugar to cover the cream completely and place under the broiler, about 2–3 inches/5–7.5 cm from the heat source, for about 3 minutes, or until the sugar is bubbling and golden. Watch the sugar carefully—it will scorch if left too long.

Little Lemon Pots

INGREDIENTS

⅔ cup heavy cream

scant 1 cup condensed milk

grated zest and juice of 2 lemons

amaretti cookies, to serve (optional)

serves ❹ to ❻

1 Mix the cream and condensed milk together in a bowl until thoroughly combined.

2 Stir in the lemon zest and juice.

3 Pour into 4–6 serving dishes and let chill in the refrigerator until ready to serve. Serve with the amaretti cookies, if using.

Caramelized Pineapple Slices

INGREDIENTS

6 thick slices pineapple

juice of 1 large orange

6 tbsp light brown sugar

makes 6 slices

1 Preheat the broiler. Lay the pineapple slices on a baking sheet or on a broiler pan and sprinkle with half the orange juice.

2 Sprinkle with half the sugar and broil for 2 to 3 minutes until the sugar is bubbling and caramelized.

3 Turn the slices over and sprinkle with the remaining orange juice and sugar. Broil for an additional 2 to 3 minutes and serve.

Plums in Spiced Red Wine

INGREDIENTS

1¼ cups red wine

3 heaping tbsp dark brown sugar

1 cinnamon stick, broken

4 cardamom pods, cracked

pinch of ground cloves

8 firm red plums, pitted and halved

4 tbsp sour cream, to serve (optional)

serves ❷ to ❹

1 Put the red wine, sugar, cinnamon, cardamom, and ground cloves in a pan and slowly bring to a boil, stirring until the sugar has dissolved completely.

2 Add the plums to the pan and cook gently for about 5 minutes.

3 Remove from the heat and let cool completely before serving with sour cream, if desired.

Broiled Tropical Fruits with Spiced Butter

INGREDIENTS

8 tbsp unsalted butter

2 tbsp preserved ginger, chopped

½ tsp ground cinnamon

½ tsp grated nutmeg

2 tsp lemon juice

2 tsp confectioners' sugar

4 halved bananas

4 pineapple wedges

2 papayas, sliced

1 mango, sliced

serves ❹

1 Preheat the broiler or barbecue. Cream the butter with the spices, lemon juice, and confectioners' sugar in a large bowl.

2 Spread half of the spicy butter mixture over the pieces of fruit.

3 Place the fruit on the broiler rack and broil for 2 to 3 minutes until beginning to caramelize.

4 Turn the fruit over and repeat with the remaining mixture. Serve.

Cherry Mascarpone Creams

INGREDIENTS

15 oz/425 g canned black
cherries in syrup, pitted

1 tbsp rose water

2½ cups mascarpone cheese

slivered toasted almonds or
chopped pistachios,
to decorate

serves 4

1 Drain the cherries and set aside 2
tablespoons of the syrup.

2 Stir the rose water into the reserved cherry
syrup, then stir into the cherries.

3 Spoon into 4 serving dishes. Cover with the
mascarpone and sprinkle with the almonds or
pistachios. Let chill in the refrigerator until
ready to serve.

Orange & Caramel Bananas

INGREDIENTS

½ cup granulated
or superfine sugar

1 tsp vanilla extract

finely grated zest and
juice of 1 orange

4 bananas, peeled
and thickly sliced

2 tbsp butter

ice cream of your choice, to
serve (optional)

serves 4

1 Put the sugar, vanilla extract, and orange juice in a skillet and heat gently until it forms a caramel.

2 Add the banana slices and cook, shaking the skillet, for 1 to 2 minutes until they are coated with the caramel.

3 Add the butter to the skillet and cook for an additional 3 minutes shaking the skillet to coat the bananas.

4 Tip the bananas onto a serving plate and sprinkle with the orange zest. Serve hot with the ice cream, if using.

7 Desserts

Finishing touches make a huge difference to the appearance of desserts. Crushed cookies, finely grated citrus zest, or chocolate curls make impressive decorations. To make chocolate curls, use a vegetable peeler to shave off long pieces from a chocolate bar. A quick dusting of confectioners' sugar, sifted over desserts just before serving, also adds a stylish finish.

Brown Sugar Mocha Cream Dessert

INGREDIENTS

1¼ cups heavy cream

1 tsp vanilla extract

1¾ cups fresh whole wheat breadcrumbs

scant ½ cup dark brown sugar

1 tbsp instant coffee granules

2 tbsp unsweetened cocoa

grated chocolate, to decorate (optional)

serves 4 to 6

1 Whip the cream and vanilla extract together in a large bowl until thick and softly peaking.

2 Mix the breadcrumbs, sugar, coffee, and cocoa together in another large bowl and layer the dry mixture with the whipped cream in serving glasses, ending with whipped cream. Sprinkle with grated chocolate, if using.

3 Cover tightly and let chill in the refrigerator for several hours, or overnight, before serving.

Ginger Baked Alaskas

INGREDIENTS

4 tbsp golden raisins or raisins

3 tbsp dark rum or ginger wine

4 square slices ginger cake

4 scoops vanilla ice cream or
rum and raisin ice cream

3 egg whites

scant 1 cup granulated
or superfine sugar

serves ❹

1 Preheat the oven to 450°F/230°C. Mix the golden raisins with the rum in a small bowl.

2 Place the cake slices well apart on a baking sheet and scatter a spoonful of the soaked golden raisins on each slice.

3 Place a scoop of ice cream in the center of each slice and place in the freezer.

4 Meanwhile, whisk the egg whites in a large grease-free bowl until soft peaks form then gradually whisk the sugar into the egg whites, a tablespoonful at a time, until the mixture forms stiff peaks.

5 Remove the ice cream-topped cake slices from the freezer and spoon the meringue mixture over the ice cream. Spread to cover the ice cream completely.

6 Bake in the oven for about 5 minutes until starting to brown. Serve immediately.

No-Bake Chocolate Fudge Cake

INGREDIENTS

8 oz/225 g semisweet chocolate

1 cup unsalted butter

3 tbsp black coffee

¼ cup light brown sugar

few drops of vanilla extract

8 oz/225 g graham crackers, crushed

½ cup raisins

¾ cup walnuts, chopped

serves 6 to 8

1 Line a 1-lb/450-g loaf pan or an 8-inch/20-cm round cake pan with wax paper or nonstick parchment paper. Melt the chocolate, butter, coffee, sugar, and vanilla extract in a pan over low heat.

2 Add the crushed crackers, raisins, and walnuts and stir well.

3 Spoon the mixture into the prepared loaf pan.

4 Let set and then refrigerate for an hour. When ready to serve, turn out and cut into thin slices.

White Wine & Honey Syllabub

INGREDIENTS

3 tbsp brandy

3 tbsp white wine

2½ cups heavy cream

6 tbsp honey

½ cup slivered almonds

serves 4 to 6

1 Combine the brandy and white wine in a bowl.

2 Whip the cream in a large bowl until just thickened.

3 Add the honey to the cream and whip again for about 15 seconds.

4 Pour the brandy and wine mixture in a continuous stream onto the cream and honey mixture, whisking continuously until all the liquid is absorbed and the mixture forms soft peaks.

5 Spoon into serving dishes and let chill in the refrigerator for 2 to 3 hours.

6 Just before serving scatter over the almonds.

Jamaican Cream

INGREDIENTS

1¼ cups heavy cream

2 tbsp light brown sugar

1 tbsp strong coffee or coffee liqueur

2 tbsp dark rum

2 ripe bananas

chocolate-covered coffee beans, to decorate

serves ❷

1 Whip the cream, sugar, and coffee together in a large bowl until thick and softly peaking.

2 Gradually fold in the rum.

3 Peel and slice the bananas, then gently stir into the mixture.

4 Spoon into serving glasses or bowls and top with chocolate-covered coffee beans. Let chill until ready to serve.

Cheat's Chocolate Pots

INGREDIENTS

5 oz/140 g good-quality semisweet chocolate, at least 60% cocoa solids, broken into small pieces or chopped

1¾ cups heavy cream

1 tsp vanilla extract

serves ❹ to ❻

1 Melt the chocolate in a bowl set over a pan of simmering, not boiling, water, or melt in a glass or ceramic bowl in a microwave oven.

2 Remove the bowl from the pan or microwave and gradually stir in the cream and vanilla extract until the mixture is smooth.

3 Pour into small coffee cups or dishes and let chill in the refrigerator until ready to serve.

Mocha Creams

INGREDIENTS

12 marshmallows

½ cup strong black coffee

2 oz/55 g semisweet chocolate, finely chopped or grated

1¼ cups heavy cream

serves ❷ to ❹

1 Put the marshmallows in a pan with the coffee and half the chocolate. Heat gently until melted. Remove the pan from the heat.

2 Whip the cream in a large bowl until thick and softly peaking, then gently stir in the coffee mixture.

3 Spoon into 2–4 serving bowls or dishes and sprinkle with the remaining chocolate. Let chill in the refrigerator until ready to serve.

Index